GRANNY DOES EUROPE:
A Love Story

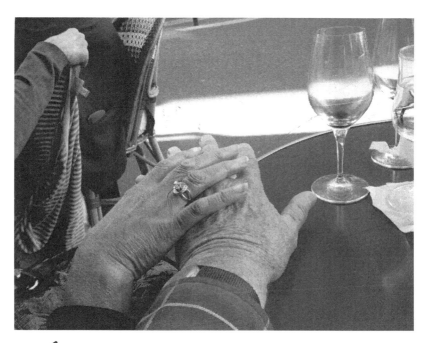

ALICIA SCHOOLER-HUGG

Contents

Introduction

When the dating service first brought him to my attention, I was favorably impressed by Cecil Cutting's profile. He'd posted several photographs, one of which showed him sipping wine with his son, and I am a wine enthusiast. I liked that he was tall, loved traveling and reading, and had an engaging smile. But I ruled him out as a potential match primarily because he was a pilot who not only flew small planes, but also built them, and I had a serious flying phobia.

After studying the photo of him standing beside a small plane he'd built, I concluded that he wouldn't be interested in me anyway and was probably looking for a woman pilot or someone interested in small aircraft. I have always had difficulty boarding even commercial jets, and the thought of flying in a small plane terrified me. Further, his online handle, "36CCC," led me to believe he was a "breast man," and I, with a mere A-plus or B-minus cup, was certainly no match for him in that category.

I needn't have worried. It turned out that CCC represented his full name—Cecil Cooper Cutting—and '36 was the year of his birth. That it was an interracial match—I'm black/mixed race, and he is white—was also a consideration, but not a deal breaker. I had just posted my profile, dated only one other man—a "recovering alcoholic"—and was hesitant but curious when he contacted me online, suggesting we meet.

"You're a writer," he said, "and I'm a reader. Let's meet." His telephone number accompanied the message.

Cecil lost his beloved wife of fifty years, Anne, about two years before we met. I have also experienced and understand the consequences of spousal loss through divorce and widowhood. We're both accustomed to having a pal, someone to share the daily minutiae of our lives with, someone who validates our own existence, someone who cares. He jokes that he "interviewed" more than twenty candidates before I got the job.

We met on a Thursday afternoon in early January at Fresh, a boutique café near my home in Santa Rosa. Shafts of sunlight penetrated the afternoon shadows inside the restaurant, and I squinted to become accustomed to its interior dimness. A tall, white-haired figure with his back to me stood in the foyer, hands in pockets, checking out the eclectic collection of pottery, serving utensils, and bottled foodstuffs for sale.

"You must be Cecil," I said, poking him in the back. Startled, he turned around.

"That's me!" he returned, grinning widely.

For the next two hours, over wine and snacks, we interviewed one another, disclosing family, educational, and workplace vital statistics.

"How old did you say you were?" he asked at one point.

"I'm just three years younger than you," I said. "I always chop five years off my age to avoid being matched with some old geezer limping behind his walker."

"Well, how come you don't have any wrinkles?"

Black don't crack, the common response by persons of color to such observations, was the thought that came to my mind, but instead I replied, "Genetics, I guess. I'm just lucky."

Something about his manner—I think it was his keen wit and easy sense of humor—connected with my own, and as he walked me to my car, I remembered having a copy of my book, *The Art and Soul of Jazz: A Tribute to Charles Mingus Jr.,* in the trunk and offered to lend it to him. The book was a collaborative effort between my sister and me to honor our late uncle, a famous jazz musician.

As I handed him the 233-page book, he took me in his arms and surprised me with a good-bye kiss. New at the dating game, I recalled that my other date had also stolen a kiss upon escorting me back to my car. *Maybe I'm just behind the times*, I thought. *Better get with it, old girl!*

The frenetic barking of a dog eclipsed the moment. Unknowingly, I'd parked next to his car, and Maria, his tiny Chihuahua, had spotted us. Cecil opened his car door and scooped Maria into his arms. Clad in a red sweater to ward off the evening chill, the excited animal began licking her master's fingers and nuzzling his shirt.

"Meet Maria. She's always looking for treats, even though I keep plenty of food and water in the car for her," he explained, calming her with soft, comforting words.

"She's a cutie," I said. I was surprised he had a dog with him, although one of his profile photos included a Chihuahua in his lap. He sensed that I was not as charmed by Maria as most people were, later revealing that she was a "chick magnet" and many he encountered on his daily walks stopped to admire her.

While I like dogs, I've intentionally avoided owning one because of the emotional devastation I've experienced in the past upon losing them—mostly through tragic accidents. Although Cecil admitted Maria was a "nuisance" at times, it was clear he adored her. She was also a connection to his late wife, since they had acquired her a year before Anne's death. Because Maria is an integral part of Cecil's life, I've softened my perspective, and we've become pals.

At nine o'clock the next morning, he called. "I've finished the book, and some of the captions you wrote especially touched my heart. Can I come over now to return it to you?"

I'd already made plans to visit my sister that weekend, so I promised to call him Sunday upon my return.

Our relationship picked up speed after that and we began traveling together with Maria. What began as small road trips in his SUV blossomed into an overseas trip to Oahu to meet friends and relatives, and finally to a European venture.

The flight to Oahu was not without some trepidation on my part, despite his efforts to ease my fear of flying before the trip.

Cecil counseled me often about the construction and safety of aircraft.

"You're much safer in a plane than you are in a car. Just look at the number of people killed daily in auto accidents," he argued.

"I know you're logistically correct," I replied. "But as Shelley Berman, one of my all-time favorite comedians once said, 'When a car engine stalls, you don't fall thirty thousand feet.'"

Cecil was also building a plane in his garage, and our very first excursion consisted of driving south to an airplane manufacturing plant in Santa Margarita to check out plane engines. His close friends extolled his competency as a pilot. An engineer by profession, he showed me pictures of six airplanes he'd built over a forty-year period. On the flight to Honolulu, he calmed my fears through reassuring words and the shelter of his arms. By the time we returned to the mainland, I was almost convinced that my fear of flying was baseless.

Considering our ages—we're both in our seventies—and realizing that our forever is far different from that of younger couples, we agreed to make the European journey while we still had enough of ourselves left to enjoy it. With the aid of a capable travel agent who understood the challenges facing senior travelers and the additional factor of a new relationship, we forged ahead.

The trip, in September 2011, sealed our relationship. We learned details about one another that confirmed our initial attraction and bound us together as tightly as the symbolic padlocks we attached to a bridge spanning the River Seine near the Notre Dame Cathedral in Paris.

THE PICTURE I USED TO LURE HIM IN…NOTE THE WINE GLASS AND HEAD TILT TO OBSCURE TELLTALE AGING CLUES! CECIL ADMITTED THAT THIS PICTURE MADE HIM WONDER WHAT IT WOULD BE LIKE TO KISS ME.

Thursday, September 8 — Day 1

We arrived at San Francisco International Airport at eleven o'clock after hitching a ride from Cecil's home in St .Helena with his daughter-in-law Anne. Although our plane was not scheduled to depart until two in the afternoon, we headed straight for the checkpoint. Knowing Cecil's defibrillator would activate the alarm, he alerted the checkers of his need for a body search. His facial expression reflected patience, resignation, and amusement as the heavyweight male checker frisked his six-foot four-inch frame. I was so absorbed watching his inspection, I forgot to retrieve my favorite lavender cape from a holding receptacle; I imagine it now envelops the body of some SFO employee.

After lunch, we boarded our Amsterdam-bound KLM Royal Dutch jumbo jet and squeezed into our assigned seats in its middle section. Cecil had ruled out upgrading to pricier, more comfortable seats, and both women at either end of the four-seat middle section declined his request to exchange seats so that one of us could sit on the aisle. Our flight attendant had tried earlier to honor my request for seat upgrades, but the plane, carrying some four hundred passengers, was filled to the rafters.

We were sandwiched between an elderly woman at Cecil's right, who immediately tried to engage him in conversation, and an amiable middle-aged woman, whose partner was seated across the aisle to our left. To politely avert the persistent chatter of his seatmate, Cecil removed his hearing aids.

"We're going to Tanzania on Safari," my neighbor enthused as we waited for takeoff. Her matter-of-fact demeanor helped ease my continuing anxiety about flying. (I later learned that an overcrowded ship sank in Tanzanian waters, drowning some 187 people, and hoped she and her partner were not among its victims.)

Our trip to Amsterdam was fairly smooth as we tracked our way, via tiny individual screens mounted on the seatbacks in front of us, across the United States to Canada, over the snow-covered islands of Greenland and Iceland, and across the Atlantic.

Friday, September 9 — Day 2

We landed in Amsterdam through a heavy cloud cover around nine in the morning. After a three-hour layover, our flight to Paris's Charles de Gaulle Airport in a smaller KLM jet took less than an hour through skies still covered by clouds, which boosted my anxiety level. A window seat and an antianxiety pill enabled brief naps. On descent, Cecil, always the pilot, craned his neck for a better view.

"Sounds like the landing gear isn't going down fast enough," he commented, sending the fear signal to my brain.

"What?" I asked, feeling stirrings of panic in my gut.

"Oh, I'm mistaken, they're down now. Don't worry, sweetheart, we're fine," he corrected as the tires hit the runway with that familiar thud.

Paris, France

Ah, Paris! Here we were at last. Scenes from romantic old Parisian movies gripped my mind's eye. Any minute now, Leslie Caron would come dancing down the runway with Gene Kelly; I'd spot Sidney Poitier embracing Diahann Carroll or Maurice Chevalier greeting us in song. Instead, scores of people, enveloped in that air of preoccupation shared by city-dwellers everywhere, rushed past us in the airport terminal, unaware that an older woman from the heart of California's wine country had arrived in the City of Lights with her new love.

Undaunted by the swarms of passersby, Cecil insisted we use the Metro subway to reach our downtown hotel.

"Taxis cost too much, hon," he explained. Dreading the thought of turnstiles and tickets, I offered to pay the cab fare to our hotel. He refused, stating, "That's your money, and you'll need it."

I'd learned to trust Cecil's judgment. He'd not misled me so far throughout our eight-month relationship. Here was a manly man. I'd endured my share of weaklings.

That said, he approached an English-speaking Frenchman using the machines in the airport railway access terminal and successfully purchased two tickets. Before the trip I'd researched traveling tips and cut our luggage down to a wheeled suitcase each and a handbag and backpack for our essentials.

I'd never used a subway and was surprised when my joints protested the simple act of descending its steep stone stairways. Counting each step, some twenty-one for each flight, helped ease this task by creating a sense of victory on reaching the end. Other obstacles included depositing tickets in their proper slots and joining other travelers boarding and alighting from trains without conductors. But soon we were speeding toward Paris on the RER express train.

Even in this romantic city, multicolored graffiti decorated the railway's concrete walls, sending my already heightened senses soaring.

"I think the taggers should be commended for the neatness and artistry of their messages—and no profanity!" I observed.

"How do you know they're not using profanity? You don't speak French!" He had a point there.

As we sped along, I took in the city scenes: well-maintained old homes, multistoried apartment buildings punctuating the skyline, and people performing the mundane challenges of staying alive.

Continuing on, black people naturally caught my eye. There were French-speaking Africans in flowing robes and regular garb. Several black students carrying books boarded our train, their youth shining out of newly emerged adult bodies. Some passengers eyed us unkindly since we were taking up so much space with our luggage. One agile young woman had to climb over our luggage to seat herself next to me.

Finally we reached the exit closest to our hotel, the Luxembourg, and Cecil effortlessly lugged our baggage up the steep steps and onto the street bordering the Luxembourg Gardens.

"Just follow me, I know where I'm going," he directed.

Hotel Michelet Odeon

The Hotel Michelet Odeon, located at 6 Place de l'Odeon, was one in which he and Anne had stayed. Clean, small, efficient rooms with an upgraded shower earned its two-star rating.

"A two-star rating in Paris is equal to at least a three- or four-star rating in the US," Cecil assured me.

The manager gave us a key with instructions to turn it in every time we left the hotel. A small elevator conveyed us to our fourth-floor room. While it was European small, I was pleasantly surprised to find well-maintained furnishings and a spotless bathroom.

Motorbikes and bicycles occupied half the parking spaces on the street below.

Across the street was an apartment building whose floor-to-ceiling windows mirrored ours, and Cecil, with an eternal eye for the female body, spotted an attractive woman moving about the rooms.

We left the hotel in search of a café with outside tables to satisfy our shared penchant for people watching. The Horse's Tavern Café at 16 Carrefour de l'Odeon, just a few blocks from our hotel, seemed the perfect spot for sipping Bordeaux.

OUR FAVORITE PARIS "WATERING HOLE"

Sparkling with light and life, the streets of Paris were crowded with pretty women, suited men toting briefcases, and beggars of every description. A gaily costumed strolling guitarist, composing lyrics to coax his intended targets into surrendering money, mesmerized us as we dined.

After dinner we walked boulevards that seemed longer than ordinary US city blocks, reminding me of the extra-long blocks of my Los Angeles childhood. Tourists, native Parisians, and a few beautiful women of color in the company of proud men of varying racial origins crammed the sidewalk cafés.

Richard Miller's Riverboat Shufflers

The highlight of the evening came when we heard music and appreciative cheers drifting from a nearby corner. The source was a street band, Richard (Bix) Miller's Riverboat Shufflers, playing Dixieland-jazz standards. As the American lead man alternately sang and played cornet, he gave generous kudos to his fellow musicians: a trombonist, saxophonist, clarinetist, banjo player, and string bassist.

But for me the group's main attraction was a lovely, old French woman dressed in a mauve cloche and cotton chemise, whose stockinged feet were wedged in sturdy Cuban-heel shoes. Her name was Madeleine, and she danced to the music in a nonstop kinesiologic whirlwind that enthralled the crowd.

We purchased their *What a Wonderful World* CD and started back to our hotel. I just knew Madeleine was married to the lead singer and said so, but Cecil emphatically disagreed.

"No way is she married to him," he declared. He was willing to wager five euros on it.

"Put your money where your mouth is, Cecil," I challenged.

"All right," he said. "Let's walk back and settle this bet."

When we returned, he insisted that I be the one to approach the leader with the question. The man seemed astonished that I would reach such a conclusion.

"No way am I married to her!" he exclaimed, virtually echoing Cecil's assessment of their relationship. "She follows the banjo player around—that's the only reason she's here. I've been married twice, and my last wife died. That was enough marriage for me. I do have two beautiful daughters to show for it, though."

"Pay up!" Cecil's look of triumph made me laugh, as I fished the coins from my purse.

"I'll think twice before I bet with *you* again!" I said, as we headed back to the hotel.

Journal Entry: Dawn is breaking, and the full moon has disappeared. Bells from the nearby Notre Dame Cathedral chime the time: it's 6:00 a.m., and even after taking one of Cecil's over-the-counter sleeping pills, from which he is still emitting gurgling snores, I cannot sleep.

The enchantment of Paris enervates me. People party all night long, and still from our four-story perspective, the street sounds waft through our opened windows: whizzing buses, revved-up motorcycles, laugh-filled voices of French partygoers. Now I'll try once more to stop the swirling images in my head, after having put words to computer.

Saturday, September 10 — Day 3
Notre Dame de Paris

The Notre Dame de Paris, French for Our Lady of Paris, is considered one of the finest examples of French Gothic architecture. When we entered the church, I was awed by the extraordinary height of its ceilings and the huge lighted cross at the pulpit's center. Recorded choir music endowed the cathedral with a sacred aura. Its massive windows were stained-glass works of art, as were paintings of Jesus, the saints, and the Virgin Mary adorning its walls. The entombed remains of several cardinals, with inscriptions identifying them and their time spent at the church, and the glittering candles throughout captured my imagination.

Tour guides spewed facts about the cathedral in several languages. For additional fees, visitors could access sections of the chapel not available to nonpaying tourists. Tourists occupied the pews, and for the first time we witnessed something that we would encounter throughout Europe: even though cameras were prohibited in these sacred and historical edifices, flashes of light demonstrated that many disregarded this rule.

At the exit, Cecil handed a coin to the elderly nun in a gray habit collecting "alms." Outside, gargoyles perched on the church's eaves reminded me of Victor Hugo's *Hunchback of Notre Dame.*

Along the River Seine's Right Bank, artists displayed small canvases of Parisian landmarks, while souvenir shops sold replicas of Notre Dame and its contents. We purchased ice cream cones and walked on the cathedral's eastern side as its lovely chimes announced the time of day.

The sound of violin music caught my ear, and I pulled my willing partner to the source. A thin young man stood on the sidewalk, playing classical music. Focused on his music, he played incessantly. Appearing unaware of his audience, even when money was placed in the open violin case at his feet, he seemed to compose the beautiful chords on the spot.

"Gotta go pee!" announced my companion, breaking the spell.

Afterward we sat on a bench sheltered by sycamore trees shedding multicolored leaves that bode summer's end. Surrounded by people communicating in various languages, we bathed in the peaceful beauty of a Paris afternoon.

The gentlest of breezes cooled and caressed our bodies, and our thoughts turned to love.

"I used to think I had a limited supply of love—only enough for my wife and family," Cecil said. "When she died, I thought that was the end of it. Now I realize that love has no boundaries. There's an endless reservoir within each of us."

"How lucky we are to have found one another at this time of our lives!" I responded, as he leaned toward me for a kiss.

The Pont de l'Archeveche Bridge, the River Seine

Crossing the Ponte de l'Archeveche Bridge over the River Seine, we spied dozens of padlocks inscribed with lovers' names attached to the bridge and decided to lock our love there, just as we'd done in Lovelock, Nevada, some months back.

We found the padlocks across the street at a souvenir shop run by an attractive woman wearing a beautiful sari.

"I'm Indian and Pakistani," she revealed when I asked about her outfit. "It's from my country."

We returned to the place of committed lovers, where Cecil inscribed our names on the lock with indelible ink, secured it to the bridge, and tossed its key into the Seine's murky waters. Just as we sealed our "ceremony" with a kiss, a huge boat crowded with tourists, oblivious to our display of senior affection, passed below us.

Continuing our walk, the shrill sound of a European police siren led us to another gathering crowd. Thinking we'd stumbled upon some mishap, we headed toward the growing circle. But the vehicle continued on. Our curiosity aroused, we entered the circle and discovered a group of street acrobats who dazzled us with their amazing physicality and molding of muscle and bone to boom-box music with a beat.

Evening was upon us, and nearing our hotel, we stopped at the Horse's Tavern. The waiter recognized us from the previous night and brought a small bowl of dried fruit with our drinks. A slim, suited black man and a white couple, conversing animatedly in French, occupied the next table. The man acknowledged us in English, saying he'd noticed us the night before and asked to borrow a chair from our table. An attractive white woman soon joined the group, and it was evident they were all good friends.

"Isn't that the same guy we saw last night here with a young woman?" Cecil asked.

"You're right, and last night he wore a sporty sweater and slacks. Wonder what's up with him?" I said. Cecil and I exchanged knowing glances.

After speculating about the man, my companion declared, "I want bananas. They'd be nice to take my meds with in the morning."

Since I'd noticed a growing stench from Parisian sewers, I requested bottled water.

"Why don't you just drink from the faucets, like me?" he asked.

"I guess it's the eternal nurse in me. I think that smell must mean that the water here is not too drinkable," I replied.

I was pleased that he didn't protest when we stopped at a small market and I slipped a one-and-a-half-liter bottle of Montague water into his cache of fruit. At the hotel, we used the lobby computer to assure my daughters of our safe arrival in Paris.

Sunday, September 11—Day 4

Up before my sleeping companion, I grabbed the TV control and scanned the available channels. CNN Europe, the only English-speaking TV station broadcasting in Paris, was focused on the anniversary of 9/11. One journalist borrowed President Roosevelt's 1941 description of the Japanese attack on Pearl Harbor and called it another "day of infamy."

I was surprised that the newscast here focused on Africa and Europe in that order, with minimal reference to the United States, although Serena Williams was mentioned as a finalist for the coveted Wimbledon championship.

This date also marked the eight-month anniversary of our first meeting, and I awakened Cecil with that reminder. We decided to hurry along, since ominous clouds outside promised rain. Cecil left in search of a newspaper while I finished grooming. He returned shortly without the paper but with news of a breakfast café nearby.

The restaurant's server greeted us with the news that the kitchen was closed, but offered café au lait, a baguette with jam, and freshly squeezed orange juice. Famished, we went for it. The new braces on my lower front teeth—a part of my resolve to straighten an unsightly crooked tooth I'd endured since childhood—hampered my chewing, but I finished the meal without dislodging them.

Because of the forecasted thunderstorms, we took seats inside a "hop on and hop off," open-top, double-decker tour bus bound for the city's most popular attractions. Headsets provided familiar French tunes and details about the sites.

"I'm going upstairs for a better view," Cecil soon announced.

"But it's raining," I protested. " I'd rather stay here and stay dry." I hoped he'd change his mind and stay with me, but he disappeared up the spiral staircase. Minutes later the rain's intensity lessened, and he invited me to join him upstairs. He'd even wiped dry the seat next to him, putting my earlier thoughts of abandonment to rest.

The unobstructed view from the top greatly improved the venture. Palaces, gardens, homes of the rich, and a cemetery housing the remains of diplomats and renowned French entertainers zipped by. We hopped off the bus for lunch at the Elle Restaurant, a cafeteria-style eatery offering a limited menu of fancy desserts and sandwiches.

After boarding another tour bus, we observed more historical spots until the rain drove us into a small café near the Seine for wine and hors d'oeuvres. A captivating thing about the sidewalk café perspective was the traffic: compact Mercedes, Toyotas, and other cars that Cecil said would not pass US requirements sped up and down the boulevards. Motorcyclists, male and female, were as plentiful as bicyclists, and all seemed fearless! Bicyclists' lanes were well defined by painted white bicycle replicas, and rental bicycles were available citywide.

As we returned to our hotel on foot, another crowd signaled more entertainment. A lean black man and his darling son, about ten, lip-synced and tap-danced to recorded music. The scene reminded me of old flicks featuring the Will Mastin Trio, composed of a three-year-old Sammy Davis Jr., his dad, and his uncle. A little girl, probably the man's daughter, leaned against the wall, watching intently. On leaving, we placed coins in the derby hat in front of the duo.

Exhausted, we retired.

Monday, September 12 – Day 5
Champs-Élysées and the Arc de Triomphe

Despite predicted showers, we boarded the tour bus for the Avenue des Champs-Élysées, one of the most famous streets in the world, anchored on one end by the Arc de Triomphe, and the other end by the Place de la Concorde. While shoppers flitted from one pricey store to another, my thrifty companion and I easily resisted the urge to join them.

The Arc de Triomphe sits in the center of the Place Charles de Gaulle and honors those who fought and died for France in the French Revolutionary War and the Napoleonic Wars, with the names of all French victories and generals inscribed on its inner and outer surfaces. It houses the 1921 burial site of the Unknown Soldier, where an eternal flame flickers in his honor.

With the foresight of a well-traveled man, Cecil had purchased museum tickets to avoid the lines, and we were directed to the elevator, leaving us only forty-six stairs to climb, instead of the preceding three hundred steps. The stunning view from the top of the Arc de Triomphe offered a 360-degree portrait of Paris, with its most famous attractions outlined in shadow. Strategically placed telescopes facilitated close-ups.

PLACE CHARLES DE GAULLE AND THE ARC DE TRIOMPHE

Place de la Concorde

Back on the bus, we headed for the Eiffel Tower. Earlier we'd circled one of the world's most beautiful public squares and the largest in Paris: the Place de la Concorde, where, during the French Revolution, nearly three thousand people were beheaded. The obelisk in the middle of the square is one of two in the city, dates back to the thirteenth century BC, and is from a temple of Ramses II at Thebes.

Eiffel Tower

En route, the bus driver treated us to several Eiffel Tower perspectives before depositing us there. Strategically placed boxes in front of the monument allowed visitors to pose for photographs. Cecil wanted to go to the top. What else could I expect from a pilot? Terrified of heights, I protested, and once we determined the cost of ascent, he changed his mind. I suggested we ride the lovely carousel across the street.

"That would be fine for my grandkids!" he scoffed, stifling the impetuous child within me. *Little murders*, I thought, in silent defense of my impulsivity.

Instead, we lunched on French hot dogs and salads at a nearby café, and I wondered if he was, perhaps subconsciously, reverting back to his own childhood.

BENEATH THE EIFFEL TOWER

The Louvre and the Mona Lisa

It was growing late, but there was still time to visit the biggest museum of them all: the Louvre, home of the *Mona Lisa*.

The magnificent glass pyramid that formed the museum's entrance captivated us. Inside, arched ceilings and windows casting prisms of light from every angle created another visual delight. Marble statues lined each side of the archway leading to the portrait, and tourists armed with cameras of every size and caliber competed for access.

Portraits of figures frolicking in ways that didn't seem Christian dazzled our senses. Finally we entered a room filled with people standing behind a roped area, transfixed by the *Mona Lisa*. I stifled an urge to break out in Nat King Cole's lyrical tribute to her, but the guards didn't look like folks with a sense of humor.

Near six o'clock, an announcement in French came over the loud speaker.

"I think it's closing time," I said to my enraptured partner. Just then a uniformed woman motioned us to the nearest exit.

CECIL AS NAPOLEON BONAPARTE IN FRONT OF THE LOUVRE

Too late for the tour bus's final excursion of the day, we headed "home" on foot, exploring shop-filled alleyways and dodging restaurant hawkers promising free drinks and superior dining.

"I want *canard*," said Cecil. Earlier he'd drawn an airplane on a cocktail napkin, identifying a smaller wing in front of the main wing as a canard, which apparently connected to a part of his brain that insisted on duck for his next meal.

A couple of hawkers were unable to provide the requested fowl, but a third one said excitedly, "We have duck and will throw in free drinks if you just come inside." Who could resist?

Dinner was delicious and served with panache: lighted sparklers—the hand-held kind we'd burned as kids on the Fourth of July—and Mexican straw hats for guests further enlivened the ambiance. The hawker even lured a newlywed couple inside, the bride still in her wedding gown, and Cecil led the patrons in applause when the couple entered.

And so ended another perfect day. I recorded events late into the evening while Cecil slept.

Tuesday, September 13 — Day 6

We descended the subway steps leading to the train bound for a neighborhood near the Centre Georges Pompidou, a modern art museum with exhibits of "a lot of weird stuff," Cecil promised.

But first, at Cecil's suggestion, we embarked on a hunt for Baccarat crystal, a product of Paris located in the city's Second Arrondissement—one of its twenty administrative districts. Situated on the Right Bank of the River Seine, the Second Arrondissement, together with the adjacent Eighth and Ninth Arrondissements, hosts an important business district that houses the city's most dense concentration of business activities. Here we passed a number of black-owned beauty shops, where weavers and braiders plaited and styled hair. Several young black men attempted to lure me into these salons, but we continued past them in pursuit of the crystal. Heeding another bladder call, we stopped at a restaurant for a soft drink and restroom privileges.

At the Baccarat shop, we examined a few exquisitely crafted pieces before selecting a small Buddha and star, which the clerk carefully wrapped and placed in the signature red-and-white Baccarat shopping bag.

"We'd better take these back to the hotel safe," advised Cecil.

People, some toting briefcases and engaging in mobile-telephone conversations, crowded the train as we headed back to the Pompidou Centre, after securing our treasures in the hotel safe. Bus number 38, with its posted warning about pickpockets, deposited us a block from our destination.

The two-hour trip influenced our decision to have lunch at the Cavalier Bleu restaurant on the museum's plaza before our visit. There I spotted a beautiful older African woman drinking with a male companion. She pulled two pieces of brightly colored kente cloth from a large handbag, and I thought she was giving him a psychic reading of some sort.

We finished lunch and crossed the plaza to the museum entrance, only to find it closed on Tuesdays. Noting several exhibits and tourists browsing around the Pompidou plaza, we decided to explore it.

La Fontaine Stravinsky

We lounged around the Stravinsky Fountain, a whimsical public fountain on the Pompidou plaza ornamented with sixteen mechanical works of sculpture moving and spraying water, representing the works of composer Igor Stravinsky. Nearby, a small gathering surrounded a man crafting miniature musical instruments from a circle of steel wire at his feet. I photographed him and returned to the café for additional pictures.

CECIL AT THE STRAVINSKY FOUNTAIN

AN ARTIST CREATES MINIATURE INSTRUMENTS FROM A CIRCLE OF STEEL WIRE.

Just then I noticed the African woman and her companion preparing to leave their table. I uncharacteristically approached her for permission to photograph her. I'd already snapped two photos of her and observed her looking in our direction. To my surprise, she declined my request. We briefly discussed my intent, and I identified myself as a writer and niece of Charles Mingus, which normally persuades people to take me seriously. She'd never heard of him, but her companion had. She then identified herself as Rahmatou Keïta, film director, journalist, and movie producer, and gave me her business card.

"If you visit my website, you can have as many pictures of me as you want," she said.

She mentioned a friend of hers in Los Angeles who'd produced a film on Sojourner Truth. We parted amicably.

Later, after perusing her website, I discovered that she was a graduate of the Sorbonne with a degree in linguistics. Her film *Al'leessi...an African Actress* took the best-documentary award at the 2004 Montreal film festival Vues d'Afrique. Piecing together other information about this elegant, ageless beauty from various web posts, I learned she was instrumental in securing better roles for African actors in the 1960s.

RAHMATOU KEÏTA EXITS THE CAVALIER RESTAURANT.

On returning to our neighborhood, Cecil, intrigued by a photo of a kissing couple he'd first observed as a soldier in Germany over fifty years ago, decided he wanted a copy of it. But when a shop provided the coveted photo, he changed his mind.

"Where would I put it? My walls are already covered with pictures. Besides, I think I want something fresher," he reasoned. "After all, there have been many more photos of couples kissing since 1950."

Jardin du Luxembourg

With time to kill as we neared the Luxembourg Gardens, I suggested we visit them. On entering, Cecil was overcome by emotion. This was Anne's favorite spot in all of Paris. I felt swept into a time warp in which I did not belong and asked if he wanted to leave. Ever the gentleman, he apologized for his breakdown.

LUXEMBOURG GARDENS: WHERE BEAUTY AND MEMORIES COLLIDE

"Nothing to apologize for," I said. "We're all merely human, and this is how we react to the human experience."

He cheered up somewhat, and we moved through the gardens, immersing ourselves in their loveliness. A young couple asked Cecil to photograph them together with their camera. They returned the favor.

The evening shadows lengthened, and the sunset's glow created a tapestry of pastel-colored clouds. Soon uniformed men began blowing whistles all over the gardens, signaling closing time.

Cecil, feeling abashed about his sentimental transference, insisted we go to an upscale Italian restaurant near the gardens, where we savored a meal of lasagna, red wine, and chocolate gelato.

LUXEMBOURG PALACE, SEAT OF THE FRENCH SENATE

Walking up the gently sloped sidewalk to our hotel, he suddenly pulled me into a darkened doorway and kissed me. My thoughts flashed back to the kissing couple in Cecil's coveted photo as the night closed in around us. *That was a world ago*, I reasoned. *Tonight is ours!*

Paris is the city of lovers. When we'd earlier embraced and kissed, two young men had shouted to us in French. We knew they were congratulating us on our senior bliss.

Wednesday, September 14—Day 7
The Pompidou Centre

Bus number 38, sans potential pickpockets, transported us to the Pompidou museum well before its scheduled 11:00 a.m. opening time. Surprisingly, a long line had already formed. With museum passes in hand, we walked to the front, ignoring the expressions of those already in line. We took our places behind two English-speaking men wearing identical houndstooth blazers who wondered aloud why the doors remained shut. An elderly gentleman clutching a briefcase and dapperly attired in a black suit and captain's cap headed the line.

"I'll bet he's somebody's chauffeur," Cecil speculated.

"He can't be. He's much too old to be driving folks around," I reasoned.

The line lengthened, and a half hour passed. People grew restless.

"I wonder what's taking so long?" Cecil asked.

"Maybe they're letting escorted tour groups in first," I said, observing group movement inside.

At noon, a young woman walked to the entrance and questioned one of the suited ticket takers. He shrugged, checked his watch, and offered no explanation. She informed the men ahead of us of a rumor circulating down the line that the museum would open at twelve thirty. At twelve thirty, the ticket takers assumed their stations, and the doors opened.

An escalator near the glass-covered foyer conveyed us seven stories to the top floor and an unencumbered 360-degree view of the city. A bookstore and an entry to a special exhibit of Bombay and Indian art beckoned. After browsing art books and souvenirs, we learned that the exhibit there required additional fees and were directed to the fourth floor, where the regular displays began.

There we viewed original pieces by master artists, including Andy Warhol's *Ten Lizes*. Unlike his later impressionistic paintings, Pablo Picasso's earlier images displayed here were realistic. But Salvador Dali's sexually disjointed paintings made me cringe.

Vivid applications of color using bold strokes and designs—from simmering hots to icy colds—seemed a primary and shared goal of the contemporary artists' works. Sculptures inside and outside, all commissioned by France's longest-serving prime minister, Georges Jean Raymond Pompidou, similarly reflected nontraditional lines and media.

An hour of touring quelled our curiosities about these curiosities and intensified our appetites. But even for Paris, the museum's restaurant prices were extravagant, and we abandoned our self-guided tour for a reasonably priced East Indian eatery on the plaza. We dined on hot dogs and curried chicken.

If you've eaten a French hot dog and expect it to taste like the traditional American wiener, you will be disappointed. They are thinner and reminiscent of the packaged jerky hanging near our supermarket cash registers. So I surrendered my proteins to Cecil and dined on the accompanying french fries.

TOGETHER WE ENJOY THE POMPIDOU'S TOP VIEW.

HONESTLY SALVADOR DALI, WHAT ON EARTH WERE YOU THINKING?

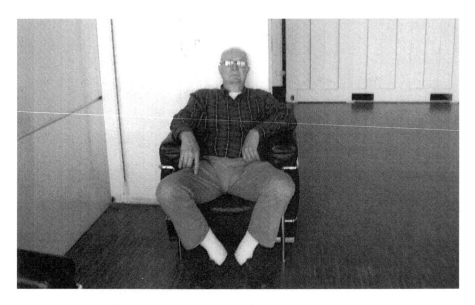

ENOUGH ALREADY—LET'S GET OUTTA HERE!

Paris Toilettes

If there is one thing about Paris that I think America should emulate, it's their public toilettes, or *sanisettes*. A boon to seniors and the bladder challenged, these small, automatically run, gray compartments, located on boulevards and parks throughout the city, quickly, efficiently, and sanitarily take care of your excretory needs. A French female voice directs you through the "relieving" experience from start to finish.

Before entering, I had to overcome my fear of being trapped inside, but with Cecil on standby, I stepped inside. An automatic soap dispenser, warm water, and a hand dryer ensure personal hygiene, and a button to control the door ensures escape. I learned that after each use, the entire toilette, including its metal floor, is sanitized. A green light outside signals entry for the next person. Also posted outside is a map indicating locations of other toilettes.

What a boon for Parisians! Cecil surprised me with the photo below.

EXITING TOILETTE

Galeries Lafayette

My love for chocolate and shopping led us to one of the city's premier shopping centers—the Galeries Lafayette. A rooftop restaurant with an outside dining area and panoramic city view provided an ideal waiting place for Cecil, who abhors department-store shopping. The idyllic scene was punctuated by sirens from the streets below, signaling humanity's perpetual struggle for survival: An accident? An attack validating our fragility? Certainly another dynamic moment defining the passing of our lives.

While Cecil ordered a beer, I ventured into several women's shops. But the outrageous price tags stopped me in my tracks. I plunked down five euros for a small chocolate bar at a counter featuring edibles and then retrieved my napping partner from the rooftop lounge.

At the Galeries's fourth-floor McDonald's, we ordered hamburgers, fries, and drinks. My mango-flavored milkshake helped shed light on why most French women I encountered were slender: while refreshingly delicious, the drink was only six ounces, compared with the *ginormous* sixteen-ounce shakes routinely served in the United States. Perhaps we should emulate the French on this one too. Whether walking, bicycling, running, most French women I observed, young and old, were not fat.

Near dusk, bus number 27 dropped us off at the Luxembourg Gardens stop. Across from the gardens, an outside table at Le Rostand Café provided a great perspective for watching determined runners streak around the park, although noxious emissions from passing vehicles tinged the air.

A bent figure captured our attention. Disheveled and bearded, an old man slowly crossed the boulevard several times, seemingly without destination. Soon my imagination, driven no doubt by my wine intake, enhanced my ever-present warped sense of humor. The combination distorted my rationality, and I asked Cecil to give the man one of my coins.

At first Cecil demurred, but later surrendered to my request. To our surprise, the man declined his offer.

We'd jokingly agreed earlier that if the man refused, Cecil would subdue him and make him take the money. "He was very polite about it, but firm," said Cecil. "I didn't have the heart to force him to take it." Thus I discovered another admirable trait about my new love.

We savored another glass of Bordeaux and assorted cheeses before walking the short distance to our hotel.

Upstairs we watched a bit of the Miss Universe pageant. Realizing that these "babes" were his granddaughter's age detracted from the show's allure, so my companion returned to his book.

> *Journal Entry: Now I'm capturing today's events and listening, via iTunes, to the late, great jazz saxophonist Grover Washington Jr. Computers are marvelous travel accessories! It's hard to believe our time in Paris ends tomorrow.*

Thursday, September 15 — Day 8

Le Danton Restaurant on the Boulevard Saint Germain, its red leather-covered French provincial furnishings typical of the cafés strewn throughout the city, provided our last breakfast in Paris.

Recalling that I'd failed to fulfill my daughter Julia's request for a T-shirt from Oahu's elusive Hard Rock Café back in May, I determined to find its Paris location. Even though he'd already planned for us to visit the Sacré-Coeur church featured in *The Young Lions*, a Marlon Brando stunner, Cecil readily agreed to the added venture.

"We will do both," he determined.

Hard Rock Café and Sacré-Coeur Basilica

With a pilot's precision, Cecil navigated our journey to the Hard Rock Café, where I purchased gifts for my daughters.

We continued by rail toward the Sacré-Coeur Basilica, located on Montmartre, the highest point in the city. After reaching the nearest bus stop, we climbed a steep, cobbled street and boarded a cable car for the final ascent and a spectacular 180-degree view of Paris. A copper-sprayed man, posing as a statue in front of the church, presented another photo op.

Seated on wooden pews inside the cathedral, we viewed sculptures, paintings, stained-glass windows, inscriptions, and candles—reminiscent of our Notre Dame experience.

It seemed appropriate to have our last Parisian meal at the Horse's Tavern. Misty-eyed, we walked the remaining distance to the hotel, resisting the urge to enter a beckoning doorway for another soulful kiss.

> *Journal Entry: And now, at 7:10 p.m., I will close this journal and pack my computer. We will board another plane in the morning for Venice. Cecil, with his confessed habit for orderliness, has already packed and is ready to fly.*

AT THE SACRÉ-COEUR BASILICA, SALUTING THE COPPER "STATUE"

AT THE HORSE'S TAVERN, THE LAST TIME I SAW PARIS

Friday, September 16 — Day 9

Who can sleep when expecting a 4:00 a.m. wake-up call? We dozed fitfully and finally gave up.

Downstairs, awaiting the arrival of our taxi, we read *The New York Times'* global edition. Focusing on geopolitical news and features, the newspaper provided a world perspective that totally surprised me, having been immersed in a lifetime of USA-focused news.

At 5:20 a.m. our cab arrived, and within twenty minutes we were at the airport. The plane, suspiciously named Easy Jet, coughed and sputtered before takeoff and again just before our Venice landing. This time Cecil calmed my fears by focusing on the aerial view of the snow-covered Alps. After landing, we walked to the nearby dock and boarded our waterbus to Lido, where, since Venice's hotels were fully booked, our travel agent had reserved lodging for us.

The Lido, Italy, and the Hotel Villa Edera

An island that forms the main barrier between Venice and the open sea, the Lido, located on the Adriatic Sea, is famous for its beaches.

The hot and humid weather was in deep contrast to the mild summer days we'd experienced in Paris. We pulled our luggage along cobblestoned streets from the downtown waterbus docks to the Hotel Villa Edera, entering its gated yard at eleven in the morning.

"Sorry," said the middle-aged blonde sitting behind the lobby desk, "you cannot check in until one o'clock."

Relieved that she spoke English, albeit with a heavy Italian accent, I asked, "Can we park our luggage here until the room is ready?"

She gestured to an area next to a couch. I hesitated, since the space seemed easily accessible to anyone entering the hotel, but its close proximity to the innkeeper's station was reassuring. I was further relieved by her apparent change of mind, for she pulled back from her computer, phoned the housekeeper, and reported, "Your room will be available in an hour."

Freed of our luggage, we headed for a downtown café, ordered pizza and cola, explored shops, and purchased water, wine, and a corkscrew. At Paris's de Gaulle Airport, Cecil's treasured Swiss Army knife with the built-in corkscrew and other useful gadgets was confiscated because he'd forgotten to pack it in his regular suitcase—necessitating the corkscrew purchase.

Hot, sweaty, and exhausted, we returned to our roomy new quarters, where, showered and energized, we enjoyed the wine and each other. We napped briefly before taking off to explore the town.

We walked several blocks along the seashore, stopping passersby for directions to a casino on Cecil's "points of interest" list. The island's inhabitants seemed anxious to help us, but language was a barrier to explicit directions. We stopped to rest on a rocky beach jetty and watch the tanned sunbathers and the sparkling blue sea. Rental cabanas lined the beach, but a sign instructed that they were closed for the season. Later we wandered upon a fenced construction area where the casino should have been and concluded it was closed for remodeling. Succumbing to the humidity, we returned downtown to a sidewalk café for lunch.

Italian women are heavier than their skinny, thin-lipped French counterparts. Concurrently, they seem happier, riding bicycles as opposed to motorbikes and comfortably dressed in bright cotton frocks instead of the restrictive, form-fitting skirts, blazers, and scarves worn by their French neighbors.

Returning to our hotel at day's end, we savored scoops of deliciously cooling pistachio gelato. Cecil was already snoring softly when I took my third shower of the day, just so I could stand myself.

HOTEL VILLA EDERA, OUR LIDO RETREAT

Saturday, September 17 — Day 10

While Cecil's OTC capsules ensured a sound sleep, they filled my nights with dreams that seemed so real, only the content was unbelievable:

I am a young woman at a professional meeting with other women from my Stockton, California, youth. We rally behind Janie, an accomplished Stockton educator I've known since we were both young moms, but who in the dream delivers words like another talented friend and fellow nurse, Occeletta. Shifting personalities, shifting roles, shifting faces—ah, sweet mystery of life!

I awoke to Cecil's dear face staring into mine.

"I've just been lying here watching you, taking in your features. You're so beautiful. You don't snore much, but when you do, it's very light. I love you so much."

What woman wouldn't want to wake up to such a compliment as that? Seldom at a loss for words, my darling always seemed to choose the right ones. But then, I thought, his hearing deficit would minimize any perception of my snoring!

"We'd better get up now," he continued. "It's eight thirty, and they stop serving breakfast at ten."

Our window seat in the sunlit dining room provided an unfettered view of its other occupants: a young woman who sorted photographs on her table; older couples knit together like Siamese twins who mirrored each other's habits; and lithe young lovers who, like us, basked in the newness of their relationships. Enclosed by a wrought-iron fence laced with pink bougainvillea, the courtyard resembled a Parisian sidewalk café.

After breakfast, the surrender of Cecil's treasured Panama hat to old age inspired me to seek a new one.

"I don't need a new hat," he protested. "This one suits me fine. Besides, it's genuine. I got it in Panama last year!"

"Oh, come on, you. It's coming apart at the seams and makes you look like a pauper!"

"All right," he said with a shrug of defeat. "If it makes you happy, I'll get a new one."

Despite the heat and humidity of this coastal village, Saturday's streets swarmed with people. A futile exploration of the village shops hastened our trip to the dock nearby for waterbus tickets to Venice.

Venice, Italy

Knowing Cecil's preference for outdoor seating, I was relieved that the only available seats on the waterbus were inside, and I gratefully took a window seat, protected from sprays of water occasioned by the wakes of speeding sea vessels.

"*El-ena!*" shouted the female ticket taker when the boat heaved toward a landing dock with a sign that clearly read "Elena."

"How come their pronunciation is so different from ours?" I asked Cecil. We considered possible reasons, as the boat continued toward San Marco, the Venice landing.

"We get off at the next stop," he said, nudging me.

"You mean that San Marco and Venice are one and the same?" I asked in disbelief.

His figure retreating toward the exit verified that the cruise from Lido to Venice had taken all of twenty minutes.

Piazza San Marco: Saint Mark's Square

We alighted near Saint Mark's Square, where kiosks offered souvenirs of artfully crafted masks, fans, scarves, umbrellas, pins, and, yes, Cecil's Panama hat. He placed it on his head—somewhat askew, for that rakish look he loved. Moving on, we noted that Venice is a city without automobiles; walking through its narrow streets or sailing its canals via watercraft accomplishes travel.

The Doge's Palace

"I want to take you to the Doge's Palace," he said as we neared the first line of tourists on the square.

After a half hour in the slowly advancing line, Cecil moved toward a ticket booth to our right. A woman, obviously upset by his action, almost knocked me down as she rushed past him, shouting, "*Sovereign!*"

"I think that means 'first' in Italian," I advised Cecil.

"Well, she shouldn't have been so busy running her mouth to her husband. There were two vacant ticket booths." He shrugged.

The palace walls were covered with huge paintings of doges, elected or appointed officials who governed Venice during the fifteenth and sixteenth centuries. Their portraits were enhanced with images of Christ, angels, winged lions, and the Virgin Mary.

Massive fireplaces with scorched insides—necessary to warm the palace—dominated every room, and placards posted in several languages revealed that numerous furnishings were destroyed over time from out-of-control fireplace fires.

After walking hundreds of steps and feeling trapped because there were hundreds more to go in a rope-directed, one-way trip to see more stuff, Cecil and I spied an elderly woman pleading with a uniformed guard to let her off this merry-go-round. The sympathetic man lifted the rope and pointed to another route. We quickly slipped behind her, though we still had to negotiate another several hundred steps before escaping.

Venice Bridges and Gondolas

"Let's go to this bridge to see the gondolas now," he urged when we finally exited the building. "You're going to experience the city as I have. We'll travel streets that get narrower and narrower until you come to a dead end. It'll be one of the best adventures you've ever had. Well, I am exaggerating about the dead-end part, but come on, you'll see!"

Cecil's boyish enthusiasm is just one of his many endearing characteristics. We are so much alike, and for mature folks, we have the energy of children. Were it not for an occasional shout from an arthritic right hip, left thumb joint, or transiently numb toes, you'd think we were a couple of teenagers!

We found the bridge and watched the gondoliers working the crowds. The gondolas, with their covers of shiny black patent leather, offered cushioned seating with bright-colored shaggy carpeting. Several passengers had snacks aboard and were obviously having the time of their lives.

"*Signorina*," said a good-looking Italian gondolier clad in a black-and-white-striped T-shirt with red kerchief, his gondola at the ready below, "would you like a ride?"

"How much?" I asked.

"Wella, if you take a ride now, it's only eighty euros. But if you wait until dark, it will costa you a hundred and twenty euros. How about it?"

"How long does the ride last?"

"Depends on my boat, the traffic from other boats, and my strength," he said.

"Nah, don't think so," I decided, after weighing the cost against his uncertainties about the excursion. The tall gondolier quickly accosted another prospect on the bridge.

"Let's get a drink. I'm thirsty and need a beer," said my companion.

"Me *thirsty* too," I agreed, as sweat streamed from every pore.

A small café down a shady side street lured us away from the crowds. Inside, a black couple from the United States conversed animatedly in English. I returned her "Hi," and we took a back table.

"Are you hungry? I'm just gonna have a beer," declared Cecil.

"Not particularly hungry, but thirsty as hell. I need two 'light' Cokes. I'm still recovering from last night's wine, and this heat has me extremely dehydrated. Why don't we share a pizza? It's been about five hours since breakfast, and a little snack might fit the bill right now."

"Sounds good to me!"

The pepperoni was not as good as that served in the United States, but the cheese and thin crust were delicious. I stood to take a photo of Cecil holding a boot-shaped beer mug, "the shape of Italy," he bragged. When I sat down, I noticed the black couple had disappeared and felt somewhat disappointed that we hadn't had much of an exchange. It was rare to come upon people here who spoke English and rarer still to encounter persons of color. I wondered what their impressions of Venice might have been.

HERE'S TO YOU, KID, WITH MY BOOT-SHAPED BEER GLASS!

The Rialto Bridge

After lunch we continued toward the Rialto Bridge, which Cecil dubbed the "real Venice bridge." A window display of Murano glass-blown clowns reminded me of Pepe, a small clown I'd owned as a lass in the sixties. Named after a lovable character portrayed by Mexican actor and comedian Cantinflas, the figure decorated my fireplace mantel for a time. But certain memories are better suited for cerebral baggage, where they remain weightless; thoughts of additional physical baggage trumped my purchasing the nostalgia-evoking figurine.

BEHOLD, A GONDOLA!

BEHOLD, A COOL CAT ON THE RIALTO, "THE REAL VENICE BRIDGE"!

CECIL AND THE BEGGAR LADY

The relentless heat drove us back to the plaza in search of refreshments, and we came upon an elderly female beggar propped on her cane. Cup in hand, she crossed herself, and her expression of utter helplessness, scarf-covered head, and tattered clothing reminded me of photographs from *National Geographic* magazine. We later learned that many beggars in Venice are an organized lot, preying upon tourists in areas most frequented by them.

The piazza's excessive restaurant prices prompted a return to the docks, where, disappointed but weary, we boarded a waterbus and returned to Lido.

In Lido we immediately found a café with reasonably priced drinks, followed by dinner at a riverside restaurant.

When the waiter served my entrée of tiny shrimp and polenta, Cecil, having become an expert on reading my facial expressions, said, "That looks like a plate of worms."

"Yep," I agreed, "maggots."

Cecil carved the tiny bones from his sardines while, unable to dispel the thought of writhing maggots, I picked at the runny polenta and "shrimp." Then, after dousing the suspicious-looking shellfish with oil and vinegar, he sprang to my rescue and ate them.

We split a tiramisu for dessert and stopped for the irresistible pistachio gelato on the way back to our hotel. When a young couple ahead of us sprinted toward the locked gate, we realized it was past our ten-thirty "curfew." Fortunately, a woman inside unlocked the gate, and we made our way across the patio to our room.

Lido's humidity demanded yet another shower.

Journal Entry: Cecil returns to his novel while I capture yet another day in paradise. Heave ho, and it's off to bed I go at 1:30 a.m.

Sunday, September 18—Day 11

"What time is it?" I asked, rubbing the sleep from my eyes.

"It's eight thirty, darlin'."

I hopped out of bed and grabbed a pair of pants from my suitcase.

"Let's go get breakfast!"

Outside, clouds dimmed the skies, and pigeons—vying for leftover morsels—boldly occupied abandoned patio tables. We planned to just relax on the island, since our bodies achingly reminded us of the previous day's laborious travels.

After a light breakfast of boiled eggs and toast, we headed for the beach. Posted signs warned that there was no lifeguard on duty and it was closed to the public. Still, people were lounging on the sand and swimming near the shore. The sand here resembled powder, and unlike Oahu's white sand, which swallows your foot as you walk on it, Lido's darker sands urge you easily onward.

Several sun worshippers lounged on towels along the rocky outshoot to the sea, and deeply tanned, bikini-clad older women bared their breasts to the sun. Cecil jumped onto a rock near a skinny topless blond, removed his shirt, and announced his intention to "work on my tan."

"Yeah, right," I retorted quietly and, not to be outdone, gingerly traipsed onto a flat rock near him. True to American tradition, however, I kept my shirt on.

The sea was calm, and several swimmers, obviously comfortable despite the lack of lifeguards, tested its clear waters. Close by, a small circle of lightly clothed young women chatted enthusiastically, while the blurred outlines of ships on the distant horizon verified the forecasted fog. Barking seagulls swam close to floating swimmers, and empty thatch-roofed cabanas, looking like abandoned haystacks, lined the nearby private beach.

A swarthy, snaggle-toothed Moroccan peddler convinced me to buy a designer-type tan leather handbag.

"Me African too," he enthused. "Barack Obama, Barack Obama!"

Even though the handbag's strange odor raised a red flag in the back of my mind, I bartered his asking price of ninety euros down to what seemed a reasonable fifty. An Italian man on the beach who acted as an interpreter assured us we were getting a real bargain. Cecil purchased an attractive woven blue belt for eight euros. My bag later began to fall apart, and I knew I'd been had.

On our walk back to the hotel, the vandalized headless sculpture of an Asian boy, surrounded by a metal cage, captured our attention. Two Italian newspaper articles protesting its disfigurement and supporting art in general were pinned to the cage. Saddened by this thoughtless destruction, I asked my partner to photograph me beside the mutilated figure.

We later learned through *Artes Magazine*, an online publication, that we'd stumbled on the remains of Italian artist Filippo Zuriato's terracotta sculpture titled *Hey?!!* The work was part of OPEN, an annual art exhibition that decorates the island with unique sculptures and installations. Interestingly enough, this year's theme was "Cracked Culture." Founded fourteen years ago and scheduled to coincide with the Venice Film Festival and the

Venice Art and Architectural Biennales, OPEN draws thousands to Lido in its month-long end-of-summer run.

The article featured a photograph of the statue before its mutilation, "dressed in a T-shirt and jeans—symbolic of the American West—pointing to his almond-shaped eyes." The writer felt the work was open to a myriad of interpretations, including loss of identity and loss of freedom.

TAMPERED ART AND MY OWN TAMPERED PHOTO

"Let's have lunch," suggested Cecil, drawing closer to our hotel. After a lighthearted discussion about our expanded girths and indiscriminate intake of desserts, we stopped for a delicious meal at a Buddhist-themed Indian restaurant. The movement of clouds somehow evoked a feeling of panic in me and hastened our return to the hotel. These panic attacks, much diminished since I met Cecil, were common toward the end of my previous, short-lived marriage to a man whose temperament threatened my safety and sanity.

And back in our room, when Cecil took me his arms, the panic subsided, and I relaxed, grateful for the physical and emotional shelter they provided.

> **Journal Entry:** *The remainder of the day is spent enjoying the local sites of Lido, and we retire earlier than usual, since tomorrow we head for Rome.*

Monday, September 19 — Day 12

A diminished breakfast crowd occupied the hotel restaurant, and only the staunchest smokers, defying the rain, lounged around its outside patio tables. The previous night's thunderstorm had soaked the streets, and residents of this pristine island dashed to and fro, clinging to umbrellas like hapless parachutists to ward off the residual showers.

With our tight schedule in mind, Cecil had already checked out. So after completing our meal, we wheeled our luggage along the slippery streets to the docks and boarded the waterbus to the Venice train station. Upon our arrival, a polite young man rescued my top-heavy suitcase after it overturned when I alighted the vessel, while I attempted to maintain my balance and my dignity.

The Venice train station bustled with travelers of varying ethnicities and types: college students, families with energetic youngsters in tow, commuters, and fellow tourists.

"Let's split a bowl of fruit cocktail," proposed my companion, still focused on trying to minimize our caloric intake. We purchased the pint-sized container and went outside to a deserted wet patio, where he deftly removed two white plastic chairs from a neatly stacked pile.

Back inside, with time to spare, we propped ourselves against a steel rail to watch the electronic board flashing arrival and departure times. At last we spotted our train and ascended its steep steel staircase, only to find our assigned seats occupied by two American card-playing travelers who asked to trade seats so they could remain with their traveling companions. We acquiesced, and the train took off for Rome.

But when two people boarded at the next stop and claimed our seats, we discovered a problem.

"They've overbooked," determined a woman in the party of four. When a conductor arrived to sort things out, the problem was solved, and we become the villains: our tickets were for an earlier date! These were the tickets that Cecil's St. Helena travel agent failed to provide shortly before our departure and had to send a colleague to Napa to pick up. So Cecil had had to make an additional, last-minute trip to her office to pick up the train tickets in question.

"Get up, Madame," said the brusque, unsympathetic conductor.

"Will *we* have to get off the train too?" inquired my dismayed companion.

"No problem, you can purchase tickets here and move to another car," replied the conductor, his words tinged with a heavy Italian accent.

By some quirk, Cecil's credit card was refused, but my trusty American Express card rescued us to the tune of 240 euros. My embarrassment peaked when the uniformed conductor ushered us through several cars, luggage in tow, to the end car.

Taking our seats across from a well-dressed middle-aged Italian couple, the man busily engaged on his laptop computer, we settled into our new digs.

"How about a sandwich?" offered my love. "I'm having one and a light Coke."

"Think I'll have wine with mine," I replied. The thought of a glass of wine to settle nerves frayed from this unexpected move seemed appropriate.

Cecil returned with tasty tuna sandwiches, his light Coke, and my split of red wine.

"This time my card worked!"

After downing his drink in two gulps, he quickly consumed half my wine.

I teased him about the knock-off Panama hat he'd purchased at the San Marcos Square.

"Why, it wasn't even real straw," I chided, "and part of it melted in the rain. Check out your brim, for goodness sake."

"I like my hat. I paid ten euros, and it's a keeper!"

"Just the same," I returned, "I'm ordering the genuine article from the Internet when we get back home." My spirits picked up at this point, and I requested more wine.

"I don't think so," said Cecil. I pouted as he explained why I should *not* have another. I reasoned inwardly that since he'd consumed half my wine and it was past happy hour, I was entitled to another, but he continued to loudly deny me another glass. He seemed unaware that other passengers understood English and might be listening. The man sitting across from us stopped typing and looked up, and I knew he understood every word of our exchange. Humiliated, I clammed up, as I spied other passengers also attentively observing us. Cecil, perplexed by my silence, purchased another split of wine.

"Are you here for the first time?" asked the soft-spoken man seated opposite us.

"Yes, we're from the US. I guess it's obvious."

"Well, I hope you enjoy your stay here. Ours is a very beautiful country."

"Thank you," I returned, catching Cecil's eye to verify that many on board could understand and speak English.

Outside, the beauty of Tuscany whizzed by: rolling mountains of verdant vineyards, cypress-tree-lined lanes leading to palatial estates, round haystacks, a circle of sheep, gently snaking rivers—all sheltered by a silver sky dotted with cumulus clouds and relieved occasionally by patches of cerulean blue.

Rome, Italy

We arrived in Rome to another crowded train station, where we were soon escorted into a late-model white SUV by a pony-tailed driver with the chiseled facial features of Michelangelo's *David*. As he passed fellow drivers, he called to them in Italian, which yielded friendly responses.

Our destination was the Hotel Arenula in central Rome. Its front door bordered a narrow street off the main thoroughfare. For two more euros, the muscled driver literally ran up the marble spiral staircase with our luggage and left so hurriedly he passed us as we were still climbing the stairs. He then drove off with Cecil's backpack containing his medications and essentials.

At the desk we asked the manager if he could identify the cabbie.

"There are so many, it's impossible!" he exclaimed. He then requested we temporarily surrender our passports as part of the registration process.

I suggested we return to the train station and identify this driver. After all, how hard could it be to locate a taxi driver with movie-star good looks? I didn't realize then that Rome is a city with a population nearing three million.

But luck was with us, because shortly after we settled ourselves in our room, the manager phoned with news that the driver, having just discovered Cecil's bag in the back seat of his cab, would soon return with it.

"Let's head out and explore the streets," said an elated Cecil.

"I think we should wait until the manager returns our passports," I answered. "My daughter Julia said we should never go anywhere in a foreign country without them. Seeing as how she's an international corporate travel agent, I think we should take her advice. Suppose we get arrested on some quirky charge without a passport? What would we do?"

Cecil agreed, and we unpacked and relaxed a bit. Soon the landlord called, announcing the return of the driver and our papers.

It was late afternoon when we first ventured out into the streets of Rome. I was disappointed that they were not as inviting as those of Paris. We strolled down a boulevard where streetcars noised along railway tracks and surmised that we were in a part of the city with few appealing restaurants or sidewalk cafés. We saw several pizza places, but by now we'd had our fill of that Italian specialty.

We followed a narrow street leading to a Jewish neighborhood with restaurants serving kosher-style food.

A clean café in front of a museum flanked with banners advertising an art festival attracted us, and we enjoyed an excellent kosher meal, with an artichoke appetizer, "European pizza" without pepperoni, water, and a wonderful merlot. The waitress recommended a special mousse dessert available that night only, and it was a taste of heaven—white with coconut and topped with chocolate shavings.

Back at the hotel, Cecil apologized for the train experience, wanting to avoid a recurrence. "Maybe if I just say 'yes, dear' to all of your requests, it will improve our relationship," he offered.

"No, that wouldn't be you, sweetheart. I like the man you are, and we can expect breaches here and there. Like I said before, our starts and stops are just a part of being human. To do otherwise would not be the Cecil I adore. Besides, you've seen the side of me that's not too wonderful when I've had too much to drink."

Journal Entry: An honest discussion follows, and I think we've ended this day as close as any two people can be. Good Monday night, dear journal.

Tuesday, September 20 —Day 13

I awoke this morning craving more sleep. Cecil was already awake, his head upright against the wooden headboard of our room's double bed. A gap in the mattress made snuggling almost impossible, but we managed an interlude before our scheduled nine o'clock breakfast.

The small nook was cheerfully laid out with colorful table linens. While waiting to be seated, we checked out the other couples enjoying the traditional European continental breakfast.

A smiling Filipino man escorted us to the only vacant table, took our coffee orders, and disappeared into the adjoining kitchen.

"Do we serve ourselves?" I asked the woman sitting with her daughter at the next table.

"*Si*," she replied.

Jelly-filled croissants and weighty pitchers of espresso and foamy cream awaited our return from the buffet.

Back in our room, I completed my morning primping ritual while the BBC, the only English TV station in Rome, blared on. Cecil left in search of an open tour bus stop so we could replicate the experience we'd enjoyed in Paris. He found one just a few blocks from our hotel.

Outside, the cool air was a welcome change from the sultry climate of the Venetian coast. We boarded the bus and agreed to cruise the city for places we'd like to explore. The Coliseum was definitely on our list, since Cecil's son had recently toured the colossus and tabbed it the best place to visit in all of Rome.

At a food stand near Saint Peter's Basilica, we split a salami sandwich and indulged our mutual addiction to chocolate with a shared cup of gelato. Swarms of visitors of every ethnicity and persuasion, including nuns and priests, filled the basilica's plaza. Some wore earpieces and followed flag-toting guides.

Women beggars sat on the sidewalks, cups in hands, beseeching passersby for alms. One boldly approached us and asked us to fill her cup. Cecil ignored her; I said no. She returned our responses with a damning Latin word: "*Muerte!*" In such situations, I would check Cecil's reaction. It suddenly occurred to me that with his hearing deficit, he was spared a lot of the details of the spoken word and was unaware of this woman's insult. Lucky him, I thought as the witch departed.

"We'll get up earlier tomorrow and take the first tour bus. I never expected to see this many people here after Labor Day," he remarked.

Back on the bus, we climbed to the upper deck. Gentle winds had all but defeated the early morning thunderheads, and the skies were turning blue. We passed through three thousand years of history, basking in the works of ancients: prophets, priests, popes, and kings. The city was a mix of monuments, with workers throughout preserving its history.

On returning to our hotel, the swelling and itching on my lower legs from mosquito bites on Lido's waterfront made me want to scream. While these insects love me, I am severely allergic to their venom. Cecil, immune to such bites, comforted me, soothing my legs with the coolness of a wet towel. He then left in pursuit of refreshments and returned with a bottle of wine and olives.

I was journaling the day's events when the phone rang. *Now who could be calling us in Rome?* I wondered.

"Hello," I answered.

"Hi, how are you? It's Marion."

I drew a blank, because Marion is also the name of a former sister-in-law.

"Marion," the voice continued, "Cecil's daughter. What are you doing?"

"Oh, Marion!" My mind, somewhat clogged by a second glass of wine, snapped to. "Your dad and I were just talking and having wine. Here, let me give him the phone."

After mastering several European languages in college more than twenty years ago, Marion moved to Stockholm, landed a job in the financial arena, and married a native Swede. The marriage didn't survive but did produce two children, Sara, twenty-one, and Max, sixteen; the couple shared parental responsibilities. Marion's new love interest also lives and works in Stockholm, and the two own an apartment north of Barcelona in Canet de Mar, Spain.

I'd seen photos of the lovely Marion and would finally get to meet her this Saturday when we'd fly to Spain. Cecil was emotional, and tears of joy streamed down his cheeks. Oh, how I admire a man who is not afraid to show his so-called feminine side! The father of three sons who all live fairly close, he hadn't seen his only daughter for nearly a year. When he hung up, he dried his cheeks, and we made plans for dinner.

"Marion's flying to Barcelona Saturday but doesn't know if her plane will get there in time to meet us, so Sara will meet us at the airport."

Sara had just landed a job in Barcelona and shared an apartment there with two Swedish girlfriends.

That evening we dined at a nearby Chinese restaurant with good food but lousy service and determined to seek out other restaurants for the remainder of our stay.

Journal Entry: Home again, we retire early. Tomorrow promises a day full of touristy Rome: Leonardo da Vinci, the Basilica, and the Coliseum. I'm so revved up, I'm sure my spirit cannot sustain such joy and will soon explode into spiritual shrapnel!

Wednesday, September 21—Day 14

"The beauty of the sunset at eve-tide
The glory of its evening glow
When the setting sun is worldwide
With its garments white as snow
When the shepherd calls his sheep,
From the distant hills away
And the world is still around us
It is time for all to pray…"

I awoke at 3:00 a.m. with my grandfather's poem on my mind here in the city where Christianity was born, cultivated, and nurtured still by a multitude of believers. My grandfather, Alexander Robinson Schooler, with whom I lived until the age of ten, was one of the five founding bishops of the Pentecostal Assemblies of the World, a poet, and a songwriter. This day would have been my father's ninety-third birthday. He died in 1994, at age seventy-six. Both thoughts may have caused my restlessness.

We had breakfast at eight thirty and walked to the bus stop under a flawless blue sky.

The Vatican

The line at Saint Peter's Basilica moved fast. Inside, we were awed by the cathedral's pure majesty. Still, there were those who ignored the sanctions against photos and kept the sentinels busy trying to enforce the rules.

Past popes were entombed in these chambers, their remains and years of service on display. At its core were the remains of Saint Peter, on whose gravesite the Vatican is centered.

The Sistine Chapel

The Sistine Chapel tour should be deemed the "Mother of All Tours." Persistent ticket scalpers assailed us as we inched along the several-blocks-long line, insisting their tickets would let us by-pass the crowd.

Cecil and I agreed that waiting in line was an essential part of the excitement of visiting these historic places. We learned that once you enter these sites, escape becomes difficult, if not impossible. Numerous tour groups, led by professional guides who ruthlessly marched their clients through this huge edifice, passed us. Some group members stumbled against us in their haste to keep up. I witnessed tired and bewildered fellow seniors attempting to take a minute to rest their weary bodies but not allowed adequate time to recover before being whisked on to the next exhibit. I felt so lucky to have my own tour guide.

Inside were antique Roman and Italian marble statues of muscular men with identical facial features and the familiar fig leaf covering their privates; female statues in flowing garments with perfect apple-shaped breasts, protecting babies and beasts, mostly dogs; tapestries depicting scenes with winged cherubs or adult angels lurking watchfully above; elaborately painted ceilings framed in gold. Christ, would it ever end? My feet were killing me! Cecil sought the Michelangelo ceiling painting where God gives life to Adam.

"Once we find that," he promised, "we will leave."

We came upon it nearly two hours into the tour, after which we endured several rooms of "contemporary" art, sculptures, and paintings by noted twentieth-century artists. By now we were dripping with sweat. A familiar scent assailed my nostrils. Could this be me?

Another narrow passageway took us, shoulder to shoulder with other tourists, downstairs to more rooms of contemporary art. A museum and shops with innumerable manifestations of the pope for purchase followed. Souvenir counters impeded our progress at several points before we were released into the exit, which took another forever to reach.

Finally outside in the heat of the day, we were consumed by thirst. Cecil examined restaurant coupons acquired as we stood in line, and we hurried to the nearest one.

"A large beer," said my darling to the busy but prompt waitress. "What will you have, sweetie?"

"Just water for me please, I am *so* thirsty."

We shared a slice of Italian pizza, and I noticed a young woman at the next table enjoying an attractive salad of tomato, feta cheese, and olives. To my sizzled brain, it looked like an oasis for the palate.

"I want that salad," I said, pointing to the next table when the waitress delivered our drinks.

The salad proved deliciously refreshing. After his second glass of beer, Cecil became romantically playful, flirting and making passes at me. What a fun guy! We finished our meal and boarded the bus for another round of historical Rome. I couldn't wait to get back to our room and rid myself of grime and sweat.

We purchased wine, olives, and potato chips at a supermarket. Later, showered and refreshed, Cecil wanted more food and offered to take me to a restaurant. Exhausted and duty bound to journal the day's adventures, I refused.

Journal Entry: So here we are at the end of another Roman holiday. (You're right, that is the title of an old movie!) I cannot believe we've spent fourteen consecutive days together with nary a serious misunderstanding. My love for CCC continues to grow. He's intelligent, suave, and, best of all, considerate. I sensed from the beginning that he was a keeper, but now I am convinced. Tomorrow we visit the Coliseum. I look forward to this tour. Cecil now snores, and I will join him soon. Goodnight, dear journal.

NEAR BERNINI'S FOUNTAIN AT SAINT PETER'S SQUARE

Thursday, September 22 — Day 15

We slept until 8:15 a.m. Turbulent dreams plagued my night:

Roger, my late husband, and I are in a strange house making arrangements to take in my good friend and fellow nurse, Carmen, and two other women I know but can't place. Swarthy Iranian types are bombing other parts of our neighborhood. I can see the explosions and fires outside, but know somehow that they are not going to bomb us because we are doing nothing to upset them.

I concluded that my wavering faith, coupled with our Vatican visit, evoked these dreams. Cecil, who vacillates between atheism and agnosticism, occasionally challenges my Christian upbringing. I woke up thinking maybe I was bound for the fiery hell that, through his weekly sermons, my grandfather promised awaited "sinners and backsliders." Could my stepmother's death on September 7, so close to my father's birthday, and my encounter with the Moroccan peddler on the beach in Lido also have also influenced these nocturnal visions?

The Coliseum

When we alighted from the tour bus at the Coliseum, the sheer numbers of people milling about nearly overwhelmed us. The crowds, the persistent heat, and our appetites drove us to a restaurant across the street for lunch, where we ordered soft drinks to cool and energize ourselves.

Hot, frustrated, and foot weary, we followed other tourists up extraordinarily steep steps to the first level of the Coliseum. As hard as these steps were on my own aging limbs, I thought they must certainly have challenged even the most limber of ancient Romans, said to have been smaller in stature than we are.

A modern museum of artifacts and statues exhumed in the 1970s was a surprise find in this ancient theater. Placards in several languages provided interesting facts about the Roman Empire, the fires that devastated the city, Claudius, Caesar, and other notables who influenced Roman history.

We walked the three miles back to our hotel, stopped at a supermarket for appetizers, and retreated to our cool room for what had now become our traditional happy hour.

AT THE COLISEUM

Ducati Caffè and Bar

Dinner at the Ducati Caffè and Bar, an upscale restaurant and lounge bar frequented by motorcycle enthusiasts, capped the day. Cecil, a biker in his youth, selected this establishment because of its reputation and because one of his close buddies once owned a Ducati bike. Adjacent to the lounge, a shop featuring the luxury Italian-brand bike and accessories added to the restaurant's ambiance. The food and service were superb, as was Tina Turner's sizzling performance on an overhead screen.

AT THE DUCATI CAFFÈ

Friday, September 23—Day 16

Despite Rome's obvious infatuation with entertainment by black performers, compared with Paris's ubiquitous black population, persons of color in Rome seemed sparse. One of Cecil's main reasons for wanting me to experience Europe, especially Paris, was his perception of its lack of racism. As a senior interracial couple who witnessed the racial turbulence of the United States—albeit through vastly different lenses—we were sensitized to sightings of blacks, as well as other seniors traveling through Europe. I'd spotted small groups of black nuns and priests near the Vatican and other Roman *hot spots*—my term for the city's main attractions—but they were obviously tourists taking in the city's spectacular offerings and conversing in unfamiliar dialects. Were there ghettos in Rome? I'd have to explore that possibility when we returned to the United States.

A couple of blocks from our hotel, we came upon a small car that instantly captured Cecil's interest. The car was booted and remained so throughout our stay. I think his being a pilot, engineer, and airplane builder draws him to unusual objects. The car certainly fell into this category, and he literally swooned each time we passed it.

"I wish I could take this beauty home with me," he said. "But then, where would I put it?" We often joke about our collections of stuff, a lot of which has sentimental value only to us. "Let the kids worry about it after we're gone," we agree. "It'll give them something to focus on other than our departures!"

CECIL COVETS THIS CAR—BOOTED SINCE OUR ARRIVAL.

Leonardo da Vinci Museum

The Leonardo da Vinci Museum, a short walk from our hotel, was a wonderful tribute to the artist, with several life-size reproductions of his inventions displayed. A room of mirrors where visitors could view themselves from every angle proved especially fascinating. I was appalled to see my rear end as others saw it—and vowed to give more consideration to reducing it through dieting, or more realistically, disguising it by wearing looser-fitting clothing.

INSIDE THE DA VINCI MUSEUM

Leonardo da Vinci was much more than the artist who created the *Mona Lisa*; he was a gifted musician, singer, architect, engineer, craftsman, and inventor. I don't know how he had time for himself—his genius demanded so much of his sixty-seven years.

Ristorante Grotte del Teatro di Pompeo

A short distance from the da Vinci Museum, we came upon the Campo de' Fiori part of the city, where several vendors under tents and kiosks sold fresh produce, clothing, and souvenirs. At a corner store nearby, I bought a small gray silk purse, complete with shoulder straps, zippered compartments, and several renditions of the word "Roma" scripted on it in letters and ancient Roman symbols.

We dined at the Ristorante Grotte del Teatro di Pompeo. Cecil ordered mussels, which for the first time in my life, I sampled. "Not bad," I replied when he asked how I liked them. Truly, I'd never order them again, because of the black stuff inside them (like oysters—ugh!) but, as has always been my motto, I'll try anything once. Well, almost anything! A delicious pastry, tabbed "a thousand leaves in glass," ended the meal.

GROTTE DEL TEATRO DI POMPEO RESTAURANT

After lunch, we stopped to rest in a small park across the street from our hotel, where pigeons competed for crumbs strewn by its visitors. Words from Barbra Streisand's haunting rendition of

"Once Upon a Summertime" entered my mind, and I was already speculating on the memories I'd earn from this trip:

"Now another wintertime has come and gone
The pigeons feeding in the square have flown
But I remember when the vespers chime
You loved me once upon a summertime."

The Piazza Campo de' Fiori

The cool evening brought relief from the day's humidity. The Piazza Campo de' Fiori was alive with an array of entertainers. After we checked out several restaurants, our attention was captured by a strolling guitarist who sang one romantic American song after another, from Sinatra to Sting. We took a patio seat to better observe him and ordered wine.

Intoxicated by the wine and the ambiance, we struck up a conversation with a fortysomething attractive blond seated alone at an adjoining table. "Tina," for "Christina," she elaborated, was a movie producer who raved about a new Hugh Jackman movie, *Real Steel,* that we shouldn't miss.

"Don't look for my name on the credits," she advised. "I'm way down the list."

Tina explained that she was staying at a nearby hotel with her mother, who hadn't wanted to come out with her this evening. She was wowed by the story of how Cecil and I met.

"There's hope for me yet," she remarked. She spoke of the camaraderie shared by her peers in the movie industry. She told of the recent loss of a fellow producer, a talented middle-aged woman who, while jogging in the hills north of Hollywood, had paused to rest, advising her companions to go on ahead. But when they returned to the spot where they'd left her, she was dead on the trail.

Other diners grew friendlier as the wine flowed, and the cool darkness of night cast a magical patina over the plaza. More strolling musicians passed by, while an artist kneeling on the pavement nearby created paper masterpieces in moments using spray paint cans. We loved his rendition of the Forum.

Our evening ended with a show of acrobatics by four young African males who performed bodily feats with unbelievable agility, flinging themselves into the air with double, triple, and even quadruple flips. Their lean, muscular bodies demonstrated that we humans are capable of physical feats beyond anything we might possibly imagine.

Journal Entry: Now we must rest, for tomorrow we will board a plane for Spain, and I will finally meet the daughter of whom I'd heard nothing but rave reviews. I love my Cecil...

Up at 3:00 a.m. while Cecil sleeps soundly. My mind once again commands my body to rise. Take every opportunity, it says, to create—capture thoughts as they swirl around your mind. All the greats did it, sacrificing themselves and their time to projects benefiting all of mankind. Leonardo did it: spun gold from straw, metaphorically speaking.

Sounds from the hotel air conditioner assault my ears, but the room is cool and comfortable. Were it not for air conditioning, we'd have to keep the balcony windows and shutters opened and endure the continuous din of outside

> *city sounds: a train that regularly speeds by on nineteenth-century tracks, motorcycles, cars, trucks, and the clomping of heel against concrete sidewalk.*

In the night, Cecil awoke for a bathroom excursion while I was still at my computer.

"Hey, sweetie, you're still up!"

"Yeah, hope I'm not disturbing you."

"No, don't worry about me, I'm fine. Just keep on writing." A soft kiss on the back of my neck sent a shiver down my spine, and my finger quickly found the "sleep" button on my laptop.

Saturday & Sunday, September 24 & 25 — Days 17 & 18

After breakfast, packed and ready to go, we exited the hotel and parked our baggage out front. When a late-model Mercedes-Benz pulled up to the door, I thought it was there to pick up some dignitary. But Mercedes taxicabs are commonplace in Europe. The driver opened his trunk and signaled that he was our man.

An Italian radio station blared on as the driver swiftly navigated Rome's freeways. Soon a roadside airplane sign and aircraft, shimmering overhead under the rising sun's rays, confirmed that we had reached Rome's Ciampino Airport.

I was relieved that we weren't required to remove our shoes at the airport security station; nor did Cecil have to undergo the thorough body search he'd endured at the San Francisco airport. Even though his defibrillator set off the alarm here, the searchers waved him on. Ironically, thunderstorms delayed our takeoff by nearly an hour, but aided by tailwinds, we arrived in Barcelona in record time.

Barcelona, Spain—The Reunion

Cecil's granddaughter Sara found us near the luggage carousel and related that daughter Marion's plane was due in an hour and forty-five minutes. Naturally Cecil wanted to be there when Marion, also known as "Mander," arrived. Mander was a nickname bestowed on his daughter by a child she had babysat as a teenager who could not properly pronounce her name. After ordering more wine and snacks, Cecil playfully wrote "Mander" on a paper plate for a surprise and long-awaited greeting.

Sara, blonde, attractive, and energetic at twenty-one, shared details about her new job as a customer-service representative with a company that serviced computer manufacturers and about her new apartment in Barcelona.

"It's such a great learning opportunity," she exclaimed. "Not only will I get to learn more about Apple computer issues and help people correct them, but I'll learn about other computer brands as well!" Sara's tendency to enunciate each syllable was likely a result of having an American mother and a Swedish father. Anxious to convey each word distinctly, she sometimes overcorrected, almost singing words ending in *r*'s or *n*'s. I found her accent quite charming, and her youthful enthusiasm reminiscent of my own exuberance for life at that age.

Soon Cecil, clad in white shirt, blue jeans, and his Panama hat, took a place near the entrance for new arrivals. At my request, Sara agreed to record their meeting on my camera, while I guarded our luggage.

Cecil and Mander-girl

Cecil had forewarned me that his attentiveness toward me would be minimized once his only daughter entered the picture.

"Now don't get jealous," he cautioned. "I just hope you two get along." He needn't have worried: Marion was a citizen of the world, full of charm and grace.

Their reunion was a joy to witness. "I'd hoped Daddy would be here to greet me!" said Marion when at last we met. She was even taller than her father, and as she bent down to embrace me, she exuded, "He's told me so many wonderful things about you, Alicia. I'm so glad to—finally—meet you!"

76

We grabbed our luggage and headed for the nearby train that would take us all to Marion's apartment in Canet de Mar, about forty miles north of Barcelona.

Canet de Mar, Spain

The train slid along the Mediterranean Sea shore and stopped at Canet. Entering the city's narrow, cobblestoned streets, lined with houses, apartments, businesses, and cafés, was like stepping back into an early twentieth-century Spanish movie set.

Marion's place was off the main drag, down a side street devoid of automobiles, surrounded by other apartments. After going up a marble staircase and through a wooden door, we entered a hallway with tile flooring, arched ceilings, and Victorian-style lighting with a Spanish twist.

The high ceilings lent a feeling of spaciousness to the apartment. Wood-framed French doors opened out onto a tiled terrace rimmed by a wrought-iron fence. Marion ushered us into the main front bedroom, which had a view of the street below.

The sparingly furnished apartment reflected her designer's sense throughout: simple elegance. The sun dominated each brightly painted space. A wall separated the small but efficient kitchen—complete with stainless-steel accouterments—from the bathroom. Clotheslines are a familiar sight in Spain, and Marion's, situated on the terrace, was no exception.

We slept through the night, exhausted by the demands of travel. Sunday morning after breakfast we walked the two blocks to the beach. Sara had already preceded us there.

The beach! What a picturesque combination of pebbled sand, the deep-blue Mediterranean, distant sailboats, and young females clad only in bikini bottoms. Children frolicked while their mothers closely monitored their activities. An apartment building and many whitewashed private residences surrounded by cypress and other lush greenery overlooked this paradise.

A minor emergency with roommates and preparations for her new job hastened Sara's return to Barcelona, and we had dinner in a restaurant without her. We planned to visit Barcelona and her apartment the following Tuesday.

> **Journal Entry**: *This evening we lounge around the apartment as I journal these last two days' events. I've unfortunately lost my adapter and will hunt for another tomorrow in downtown Canet. Meanwhile, dear journal, this is all you get for now.*

Monday, September 26 — Day 19

Hungry for a traditional American breakfast, we sought a café that served bacon and eggs. But first Cecil insisted we hunt for electronic parts to get Marion's hot-water and room heater going. At the village hardware store, Marion found inexpensive paint to brighten up one of her bedrooms and surprise Tom, her love. In a relationship for several years, the two live apart in chilly Stockholm, but jointly own the sunny Canet apartment, to which they escape as often as their respective schedules allow. Both also have adolescent sons who live with them. Cecil adores Tom, who is a successful financial entrepreneur.

"I'm afraid Tom won't like me painting without his being involved," Marion mused.

"Ah, go ahead, girl," I returned. "Just tell him you have a surprise present for him, and he'll love it!"

At the café, we enjoyed french-fried potatoes with our eggs; it sure beat the croissants and café au lait we'd had for weeks.

Continuing our pursuit of a plug-in converter for my computer, we found it at a Chinese-run store featuring every kind of gadget you could imagine and some you could not. Strange how the absence of one item you take for granted in your own environment—in my case, my computer—can negatively affect your well-being. I was reminded of newly admitted elderly patients I'd cared for in hospitals who were so impacted by the unfamiliar and sterile setting, they became completely disoriented and delusional.

On returning to the apartment, I immediately plugged into Marion's European wall outlet and felt an overwhelming sense of relief.

DOWNTOWN CANET, FATHER AND DAUGHTER BASK IN THE MORNING SUN.

Tuesday, September 27 — Day 20

Again the beach beckoned, but this time Cecil, who had sustained sunburn from the previous two days' exposure, brought along Marion's beach umbrella. Marion, stunning in a black bikini, headed directly for a dip in the sea.

The weather continued sultry and humid. I, who had never learned to swim, hid from the sun under the sheltering umbrella. Cecil joined his daughter for a swim, and I took advantage of a great photo opportunity. His retreat back to the shade and his book provided another photo op for me, and Marion cooperated by playfully posing for glamour shots.

"Whatta bod," I shouted. "Hugh Hefner's gonna love this one!"

We returned to the apartment and prepared for our trip to Barcelona.

EAT YOUR HEART OUT, HEF!

Barcelona, Spain II

The train ride along the beach to Barcelona was full of sights: here a full-frontal view of a nude male sunbather; there more bikini-clad nymphs. The Spanish countryside zoomed by on the other side of the tracks, and we saw brightly painted villas surrounded by palms, car dealerships, small cafés, industrial complexes, and, nearing the city, power plants. The closer we got to the city, the more apartment buildings we saw. Graffiti informed us that we had arrived.

"Here's our stop," announced Marion.

We emerged on a boulevard of small boutiques and cafés. Many narrow, one-way streets intersected the boulevard, spilling a plethora of minicars and pickup trucks, so prevalent in Europe, into the district. It was hot, and we were soaked to the bone.

"Let's have a beer," suggested Cecil.

Not wanting to dampen the celebratory mood, but detesting the taste of beer, I ordered wine. We lounged for a while, taking in the inhabitants of this great city.

Like Paris and Rome, Barcelona is a multicultural European metropolis. The Chinese-run café we selected for drinks offered the usual fat-laden fried foods. Their calamari, hot dogs, and green peppers all came with french fries, so we deferred to our impending dinner with Sara.

Continuing on toward Sara's office, the Torre Agbar, a thirty-eight-story tower that marks the gateway to Barcelona's "technological district," captured our full attention.

"I bet that was designed by a man," I speculated, noting its phallic dimensions. I later learned that French architect Jean Nouve, indeed a male with a gender-neutral name, created the massive structure. I photographed Cecil and Marion in front of it, but since it is such a towering monument, I could not capture the entire building in my viewfinder. Cecil obliged my request to snap Marion and me there and assumed a professional photographer's posture by lying on the sidewalk.

MY SUSPICIONS WERE CONFIRMED: A MAN DESIGNED THIS EDIFICE, ALL RIGHT!

Sara, clad in shorts, met us at an upscale clothing store in a nearby mall containing familiar US brand-name shops. Excited about passing her company's written exam for newcomers and anxious to show us her new place, she led us at breakneck speeds, via foot and rail, to her neighborhood. Her street required a three-block uphill climb that reminded me of my gym's treadmill. Cecil and I trailed his offspring, stopping occasionally to rest our septuagenarian bones.

The neighborhood reflected Barcelonan apartment living: clothes drying on window ledges, plants adorning outside windowsills, and bicycles parked on small balconies. On reaching Sara's place, we had to climb a flight of stairs before entering. Julia, her Swedish roommate, greeted us, speaking flawless English. Her looks replicated Sara's own Scandinavian heritage.

A feeling of lightheadedness, a cardinal symptom of heat exhaustion, began to distort my senses as we sat in the tiny living room. When we left to seek out a restaurant for dinner, the dizziness overcame me, and I realized that if I didn't drink fluids soon, I'd go into a full-blown attack. I'd experienced such an attack two months back with Cecil in St. Helena after a prolonged hike in unseasonably hot weather. I alerted Cecil, and we stopped to purchase a bottle of water. I was saved.

Sara chose an East Indian restaurant for dinner, and we savored a tasty meal of skewered chicken and lamb on a bed of rice. And water, more water please!

A dog encounter sent Sara, who has a phobia around these animals, running away, and we followed her to say our good-byes.

Somehow I'd sustained more mosquito bites on my legs, and sleep was hard to come by. To complicate matters, my bladder worked overtime, thanks to my inordinate intake of water.

Wednesday, September 28 — Day 21

It was hard to believe that this would be the last day of our European venture. A wave of nostalgia swept over me as I reflected back on my travels. In the morning, a taxi would take us to Barcelona's airport, and Europe's vast wonders would become treasured memories. Marion prepared another gourmet breakfast and completed errands in preparation for Tom's arrival the next day.

> **Journal Entry**: *I'll wind this up now, dear journal, as Canet's heat is pouring through the opened balcony doors and I must ensure that I'm properly hydrated.*

We spent the rest of that beautiful day at the beach. Marion provided three umbrellas to shield us from the sun, and Cecil brought along a beach chair on which to rest his back as he read his latest novel. There were more topless "babes," as Cecil called them. One young woman in particular caught all of our eyes. While her two prepubescent nude sons compared penis sizes, she swam and emerged from the sea resembling a mythical goddess. I placed Cecil's chair on the opposite side of the umbrella so he could not easily ogle her.

What's the matter with you, old lady? I chided myself. *Let him have an unobstructed view, and stop being such a prude!* Complying with my righteous self, I removed the barrier, but by that time, he seemed more interested in his book.

After a couple of hours, Marion, wanting to attend to some business in the next town, suggested we accompany her there on a train. Knowing that our return flight the next day would require extra energy, and enjoying our beach respite, Cecil and I elected to remain on the beach.

That evening Marion escorted us to her favorite pizza place. En route, a clothing boutique beckoned to me. "Can we stop, Cecil? I want to check this place out." Like me, Marion was anxious to go inside the shop. Cecil shrugged.

"Sure, you two go on in. I'll wait on the corner."

Inside, Marion enthusiastically pulled several tops from the racks.

"These would look great on you, Alicia. Don't you just love the colors?"

"Yes, I do, but remember, you model-figured young woman, I need an extra large."

I purchased a mauve-colored top, and we found Cecil resting in a chair at the street café nearby.

At another shop, the coat rack drew Marion's attention.

"I need a new one this winter—mine's getting awfully shabby." She added that Stockholm winters are so cold that parked cars are often swallowed up by its snowfalls and cannot be extracted even with heavy equipment. Icicles form on the eaves of houses and are sometimes so heavy that when they melt and fall, they can potentially injure or even kill passersby.

That said, she resisted the urge to purchase the coat. "Maybe later," she mused. "This is an expensive store." Like father, like daughter, I thought, remembering Cecil's thrifty nature, which counterbalances my own impulsive spending tendency. Another checkmark in his plus column!

At the restaurant, we ordered pizza and salad. My continuing dehydration demanded water, while my companions enjoyed beer.

Back at the apartment, Marion booked a 4:00 a.m. cab for our return trip to the Barcelona airport and programmed her mobile phone alarm.

Our cab, another Mercedes, arrived at the Barcelona airport in forty-five minutes. Because of the sheer numbers of people flying out that morning, our flight was delayed for forty minutes. But with the tailwind driving us north to Amsterdam, we arrived in time to board our flight home.

The ten-hour flight to San Francisco was without incident. I'd mastered the technique of taking a couple of prescribed antianxiety pills to calm me and enable several naps. That, coupled with focusing on the tiny screen that allows passengers to monitor the progress of the plane over land and sea, was my saving grace. After the customs and baggage-carousel madness, we were relieved to find the ever-prompt Anne waiting for us.

We arrived at Cecil's some twenty hours after leaving Canet, paused for a cold cola, then hopped into his car for the drive to my Santa Rosa home. I called my kids, snacked, hit the sack by seven that night, and slept soundly until five thirty in the morning.

Friday, September 30, 2011 — Day 22: Home

Final Journal Entry: It's late again. I've completed all the mundane tasks: unpacking, laundry, bill paying. And now for lessons learned:

I have experienced the loveliness of Paris with a real lover, not the illusive ghost of an idol flickering from a gigantic movie theater screen, or an imaginary prince emerging from one of my grandmother's happily-ever-after fairy tales, but a flesh-and-blood knight.

While not clad in the shining armor of a mythical warrior, his armor is in the form of gentleness rarely seen in another human being. His sheltering arms ward off my fears and provide warmth, comfort, and a safe place to just BE. His heartbeat, while ensured by a pacemaker defibrillator, keeps time with time, its rhythm tracking and defining each moment. With wisdom tempered by a lifetime of reverence for all things good, he makes each moment count in real time.

With my lover beside me, I have witnessed ancient remnants of Rome attesting to a fallen empire and traversed its cathedrals, where sunlight pierced through artfully crafted colored glass, accentuating messages of hope and faith—its rays embracing sculptural masterpieces lining halls with massive ceilings adorned with heavenly symbols. I have felt the texture of marble and stone with trembling fingers and tread the city's cobblestoned streets. I have passed hundreds of believers with awe-stricken expressions on their faces, while witnessing physical evidence of the cradle of a religion espoused by the bulk of my ancestors. I have seen fountains surrounded by gardens of stone.

In Spain, I witnessed the preservation of history by inhabitants joyfully sharing their places on this planet. **There is no end to beauty here, no end to faith, no cap to joy. And this, the final lesson: As long as we live and breathe and have our being, we are becoming. In touch with our spirits, we learn, we grow, we soar. In touch with our hearts, we love.**

Made in the USA
Charleston, SC
21 June 2013